PRIME CUTS
ACOUSTIC ROCK
GUITAR

Project Manager: COLGAN BRYAN
Arranged By: LOUIS MARTINEZ, COLGAN BRYAN and ADAM LEVY
Book Design: KEN REHM

© 1997 WARNER BROS. PUBLICATIONS
All Rights Reserved

ARTIST INDEX:

WARNER BROS. PUBLICATIONS - THE GLOBAL LEADER IN PRINT
USA: 15800 NW 48th Avenue, Miami, FL 33014

WARNER/CHAPPELL MUSIC
CANADA: 85 SCARSDALE ROAD, SUITE 101
DON MILLS, ONTARIO, M3B 2R2
SCANDINAVIA: P.O. BOX 533, VENDEVAGEN 85 B
S-182 15, DANDERYD, SWEDEN
AUSTRALIA: P.O. BOX 353
3 TALAVERA ROAD, NORTH RYDE N.S.W. 2113

Carisch
NUOVA CARISCH
ITALY: VIA M.F. QUINTILIANO 40
20138 MILANO
SPAIN: MAGALLANES, 25
28015 MADRID

INTERNATIONAL MUSIC PUBLICATIONS LIMITED
ENGLAND: SOUTHEND ROAD,
WOODFORD GREEN, ESSEX IG8 8HN
FRANCE: 25 RUE DE HAUTEVILLE, 75010 PARIS
GERMANY: MARSTALLSTR. 8, D-80539 MUNCHEN
DENMARK: DANMUSIK, VOGNMAGERGADE 7
DK 1120 KOBENHAVNK

A HORSE WITH NO NAME

Words and Music by
DEWEY BUNNELL

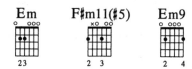

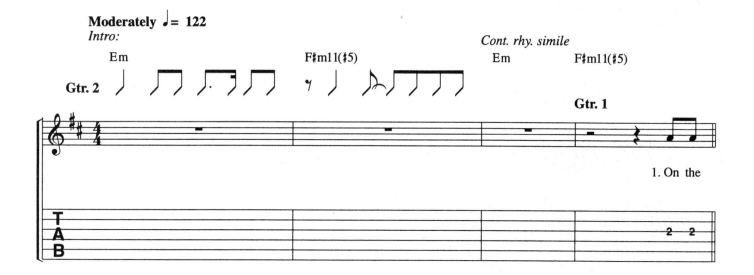

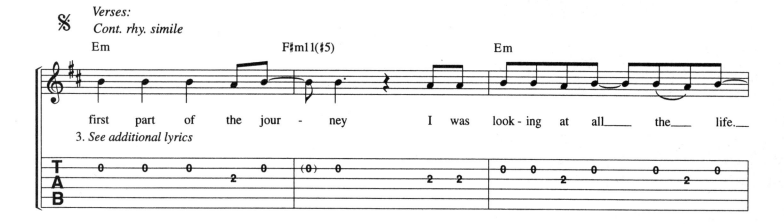

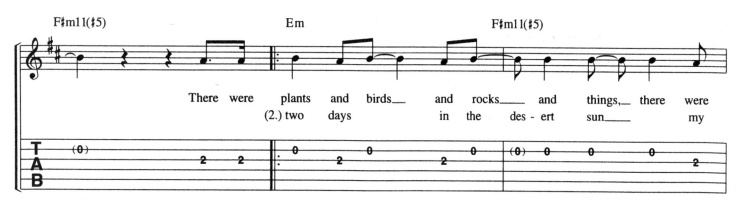

A Horse With No Name - 4 - 1

4

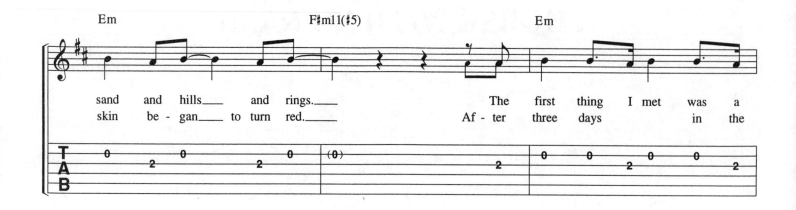

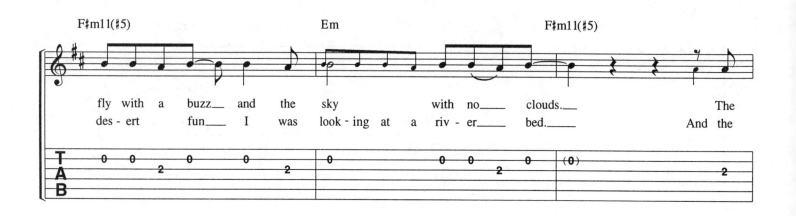

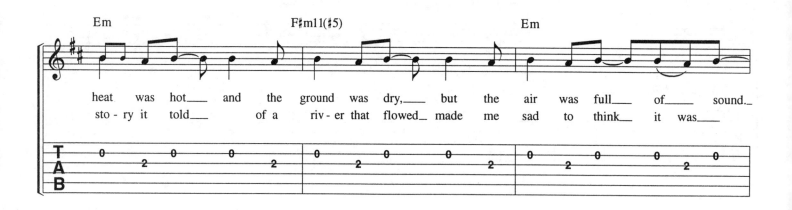

Chorus:
Cont. rhy. simile

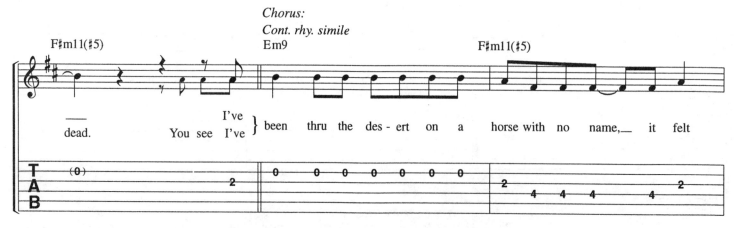

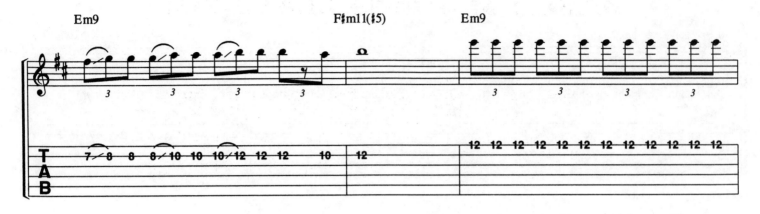

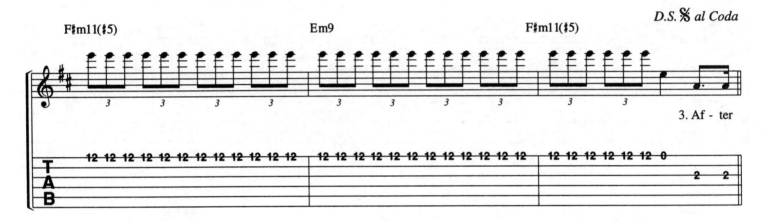

Verse 3:
After nine days I let the horse run free
'Cause the desert had turned to sea.
There were plants and birds and rocks and things,
There were sand and hills and rings.
The ocean is a desert with its life underground
And the perfect disguise above.
Under the cities lies a heart made of ground,
But the humans will give no love.
(To Chorus:)

BABE, I'M GONNA LEAVE YOU

Words and Music by
JIMMY PAGE

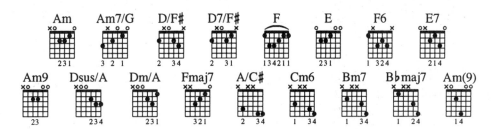

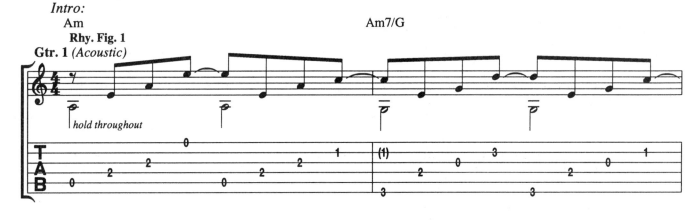

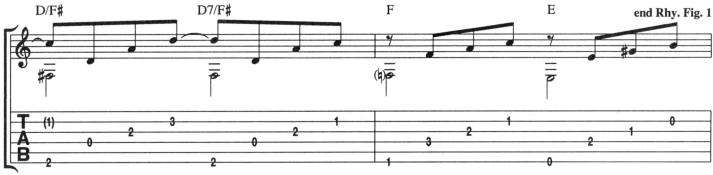

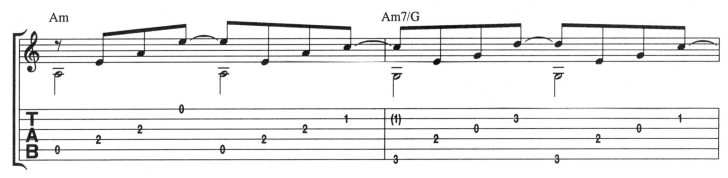

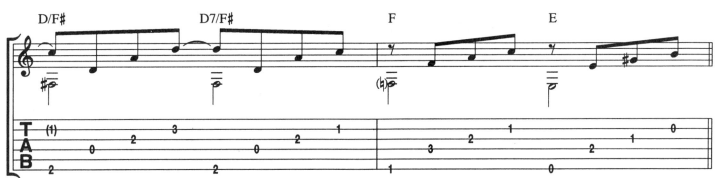

Verses:

w/Rhy. Fig. 1 *(Gtr. 1) 2 times*

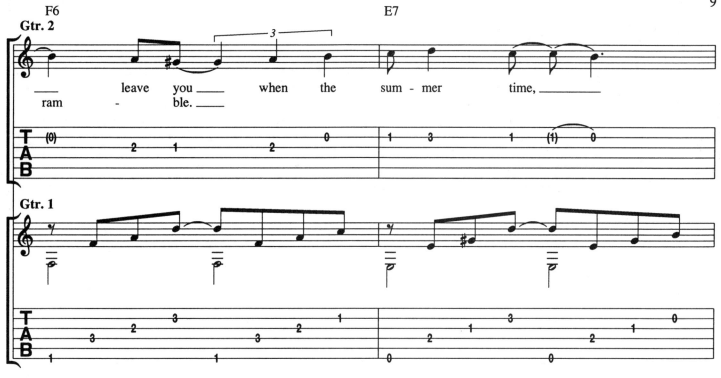

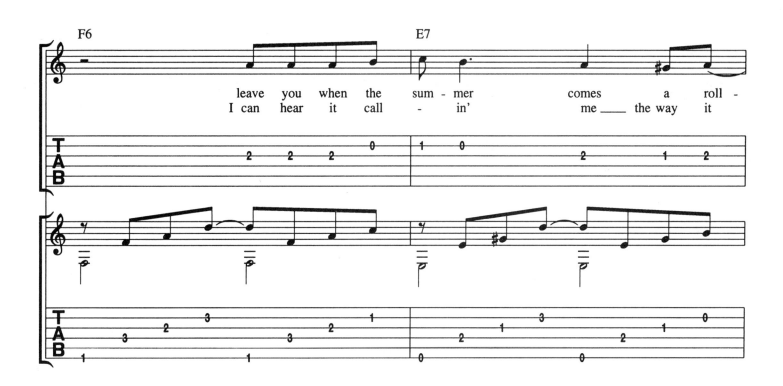

10

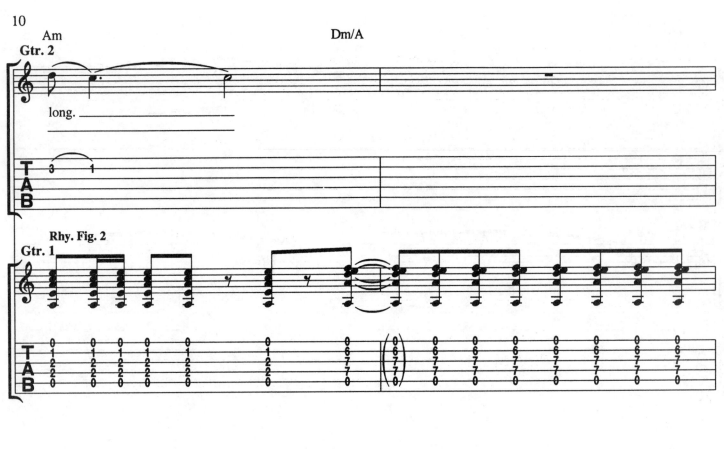

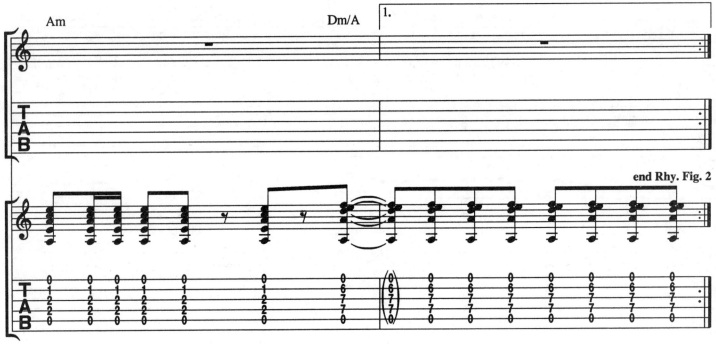

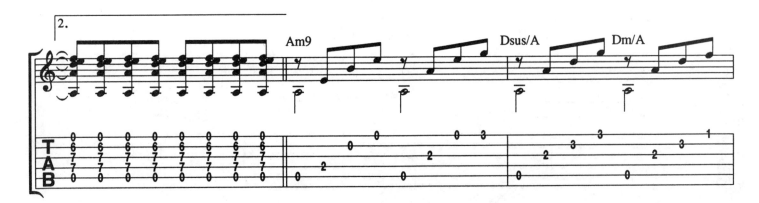

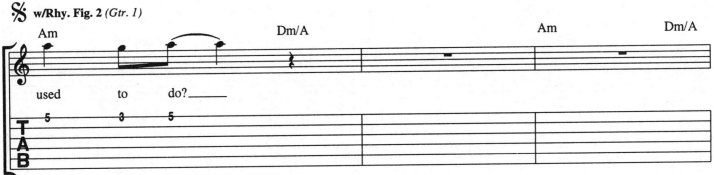

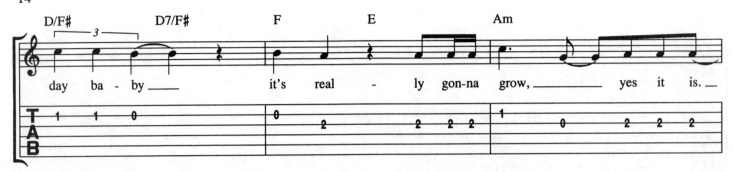

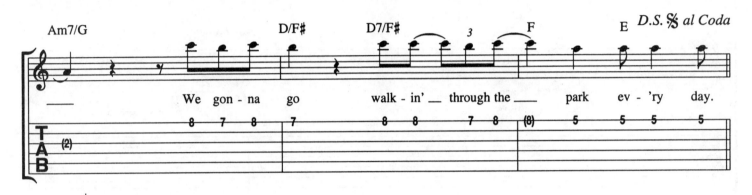

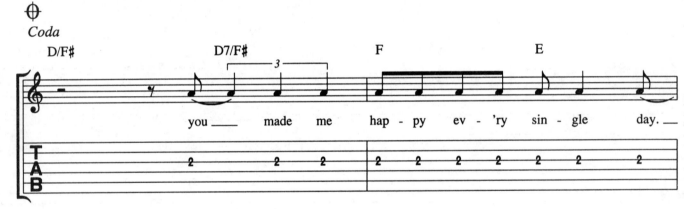

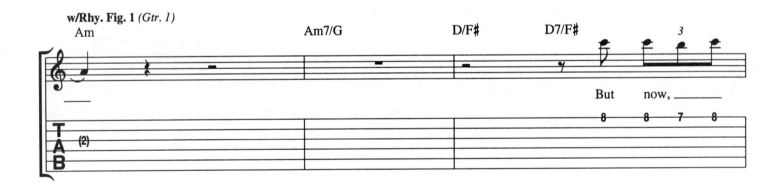

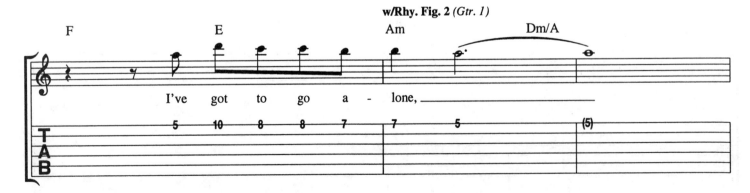

BAD MOON RISING

by J.C. FOGERTY

18

Bad Moon Rising - 5 - 4

COME TO MY WINDOW

Words and Music by
MELISSA ETHERIDGE

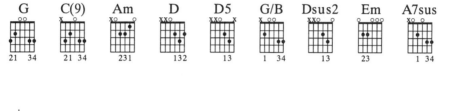

Come to My Window - 4 - 1

22

Come to My Window - 4 - 2

24

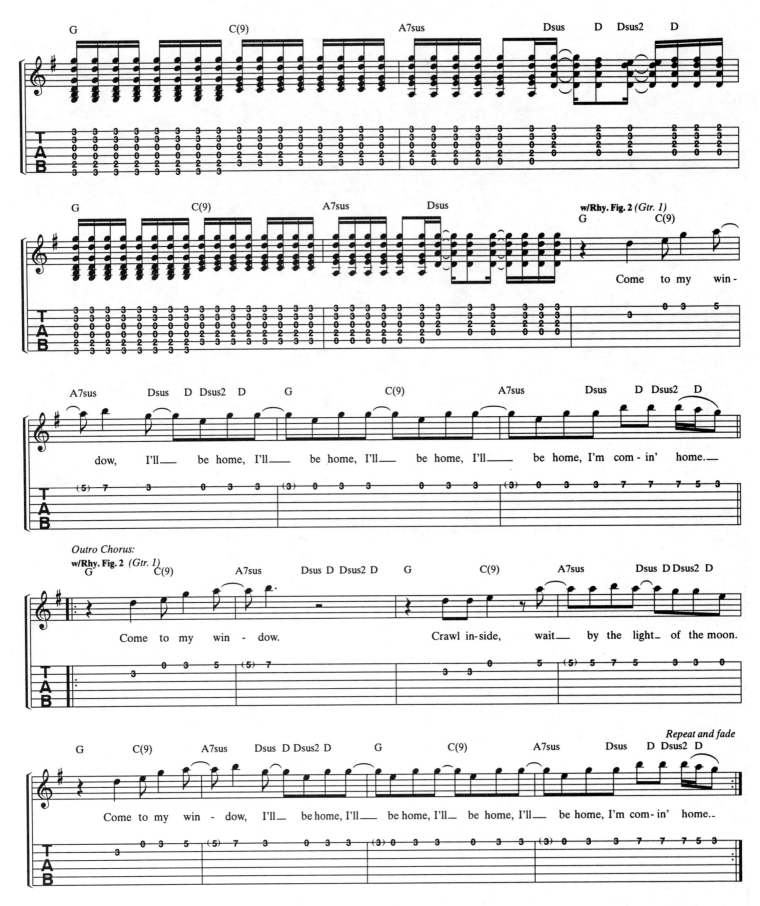

Verse 2:
Keeping my eyes open, I cannot afford to sleep.
Giving away promises I know that I can't keep.
Nothing fills the blackness that has seeped into my chest.
I need you in my blood, I am forsaking all the rest.
Just to reach you.
Just to reach you.
Oh, to reach you.
(To Chorus:)

DESPERADO

Words and Music by
DON HENLEY and GLENN FREY

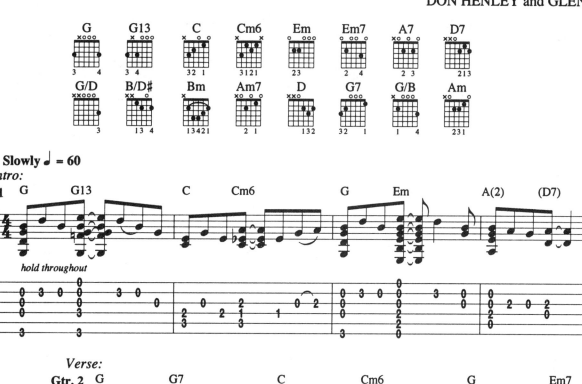

Slowly ♩ = 60

Intro:

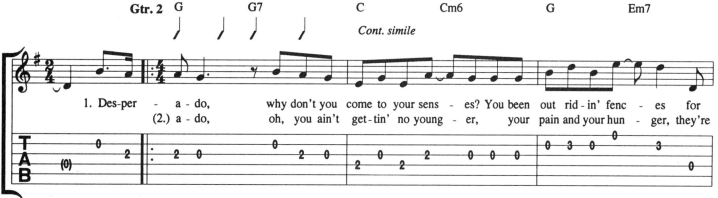

hold throughout

1. Des-per - a-do, why don't you come to your sens - es? You been out rid-in' fenc - es for
(2.) a - do, oh, you ain't get-tin' no young - er, your pain and your hun - ger, they're

so long now. __ Oh, you're a hard one, I know that you got your rea - sons, these
driv - in' you home. And free-dom, oh, free-dom, well, that's just some peo-ple talk - in', your

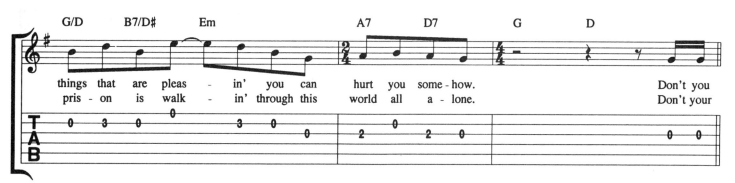

things that are pleas - in' you can hurt you some - how. Don't you
pris - on is walk - in' through this world all a - lone. Don't your

Desperado – 3 – 1

26

DOWN ON THE CORNER

by J.C. FOGERTY

Down On The Corner - 4 - 4

4 + 20

Words and Music by
STEPHEN STILLS

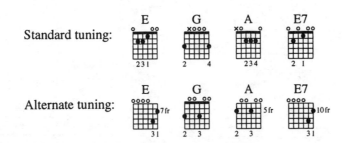

Standard tuning:

Alternate tuning:

Play melody with standard gtr. tuning

*Gtr. 1 tuning:

$⑥ = E^2$ $③ = E^3$

$⑤ = E^2$ $② = B^3$

$④ = E^3$ $① = E^4$

How to tune from standard to alternate tuning for this song:

1. Leave ⑥, ②, and ① at the standard pitches

2. Tune ③ (G) down to E

3. Tune ④ (D) up to E, making ③ and ④ the same pitch

4. Tune ⑤ (A) down to E, making ⑤ and ⑥ the same pitch

Use same tuning for Suite: Judy Blue Eyes.

Moderately slow ♩ = 72

Intro:

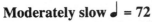

*Use tuning above for Gtr. 1 (fingerstyle)

Verse:

1. Four and twen-ty years a-go   I came in-to this life,   the
(2.) dif-f'rent kind of pov-er-ty   now up-sets me so,   I
3. Morn-ing comes to sun-rise and   I'm driv-en to my bed,   I

HARVEST MOON

Words and Music by
NEIL YOUNG

Harvest Moon - 5 - 1

Harvest Moon - 5 - 3

HEART OF GOLD

Words and Music by
NEIL YOUNG

41

Heart of Gold - 2 - 2

HELPLESSLY HOPING

Words and Music by
STEPHEN STILLS

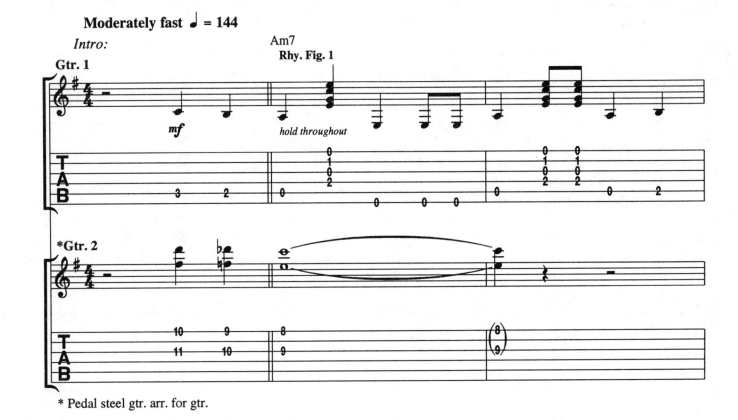

* Pedal steel gtr. arr. for gtr.

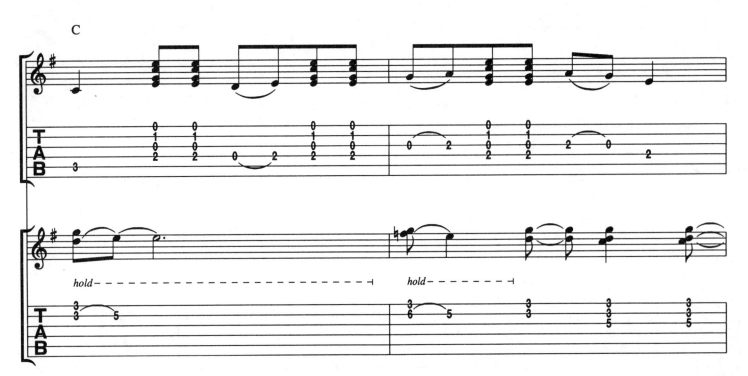

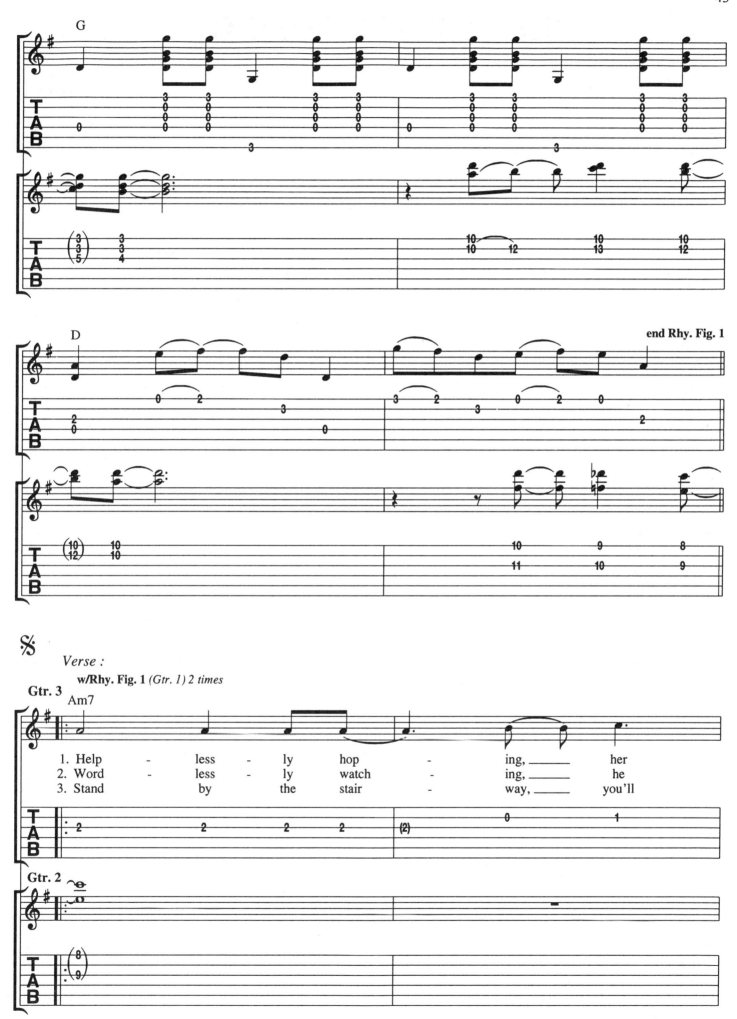

end Rhy. Fig. 1

%

Verse :

w/Rhy. Fig. 1 *(Gtr. 1) 2 times*

Gtr. 3

1. Help - less - ly hop - ing, _____ her
2. Word - less - ly watch - ing, _____ he
3. Stand by the stair - way, _____ you'll

Gtr. 2

I'LL HAVE TO SAY
I LOVE YOU IN A SONG

Words and Music by
JIM CROCE

I'll Have To Say I Love You In A Song - 5 - 1

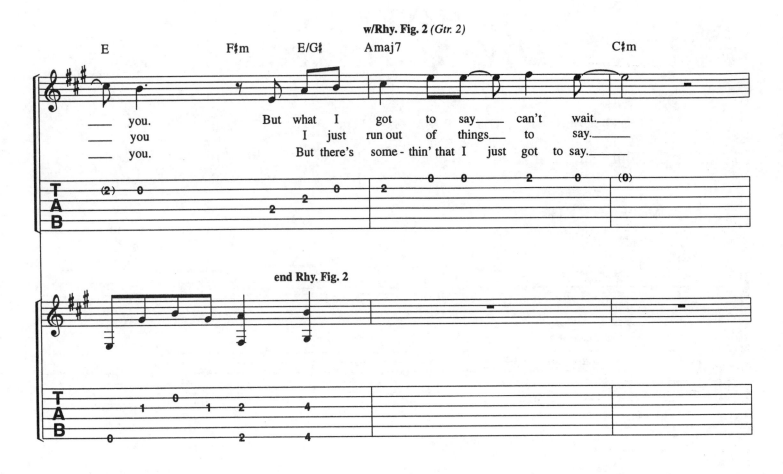

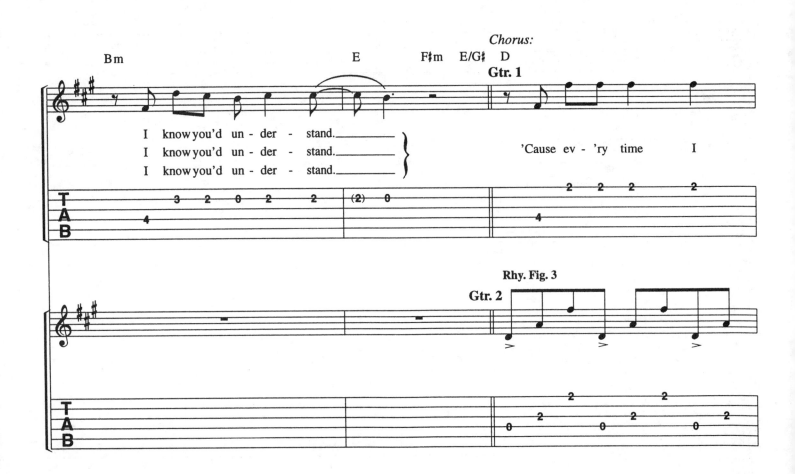

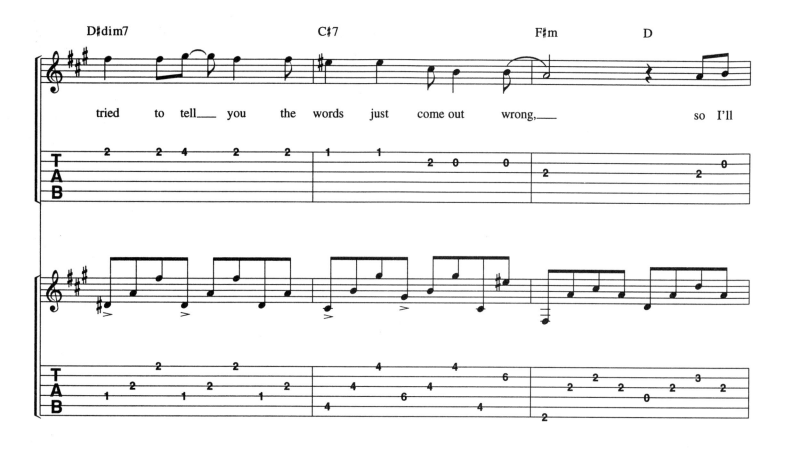

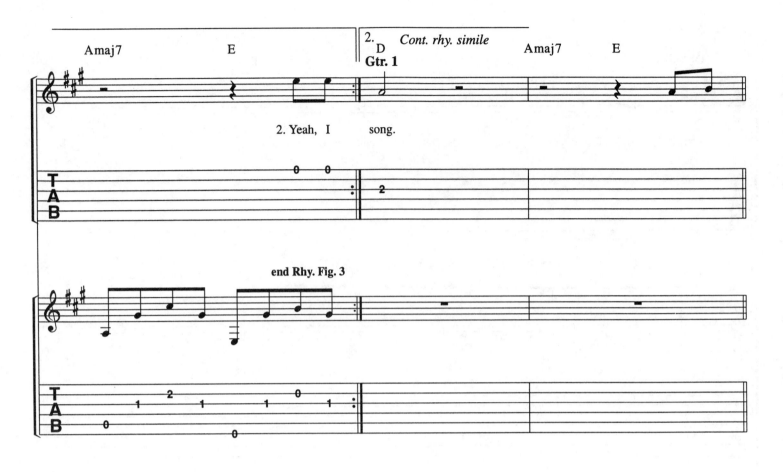

Guitar Solo:
w/Rhy. Fig. 2 *(Gtr. 2) 2 times*

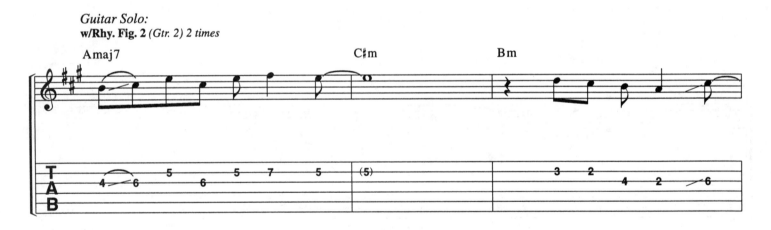

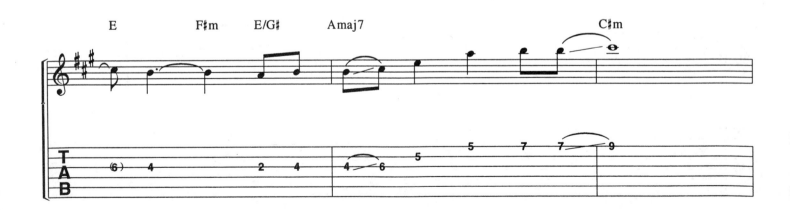

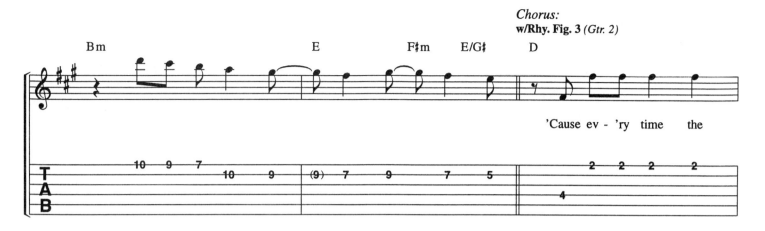

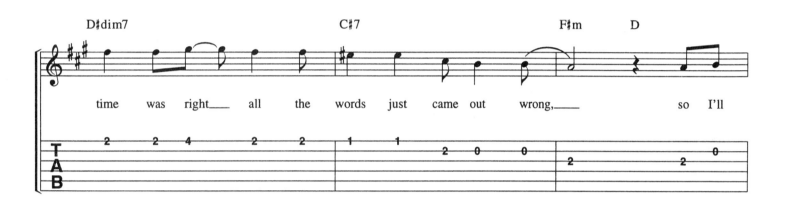

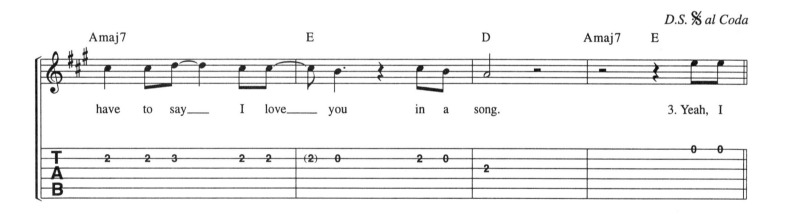

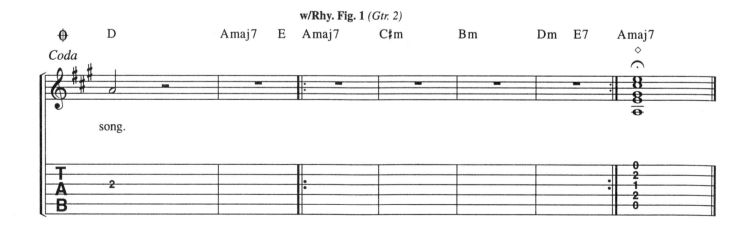

LOVE THE ONE YOU'RE WITH

Words and Music by
STEPHEN STILLS

Love the One You're With – 5 – 2

MARRAKESH EXPRESS

Words and Music by
GRAHAM NASH

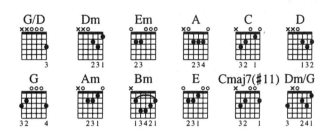

1. Look - ing at ___ the world ___ through the sun - set in ___ your eyes. ___
2. Sweep - ing cob - webs from _____ the edg - es of ___ my mind, ___
3. Take the train _ from Cas - a - blan - ca go - ing south, ___

OLD MAN

Words and Music by
NEIL YOUNG

Old Man - 3 - 1

OPERATOR
(THAT'S NOT THE WAY IT FEELS)

Words and Music by
JIM CROCE

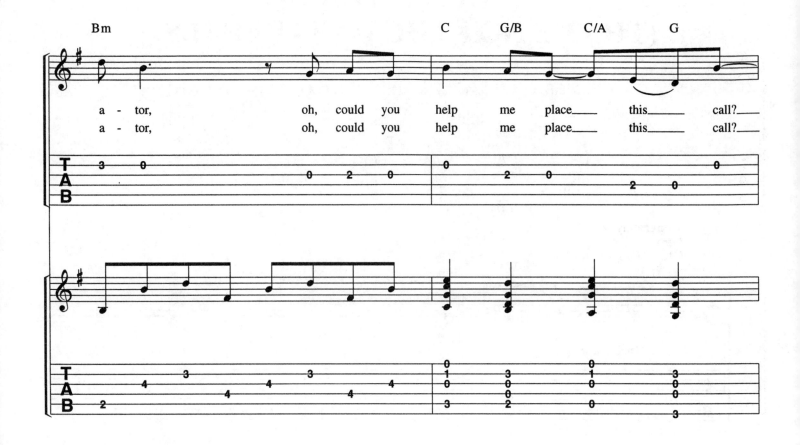

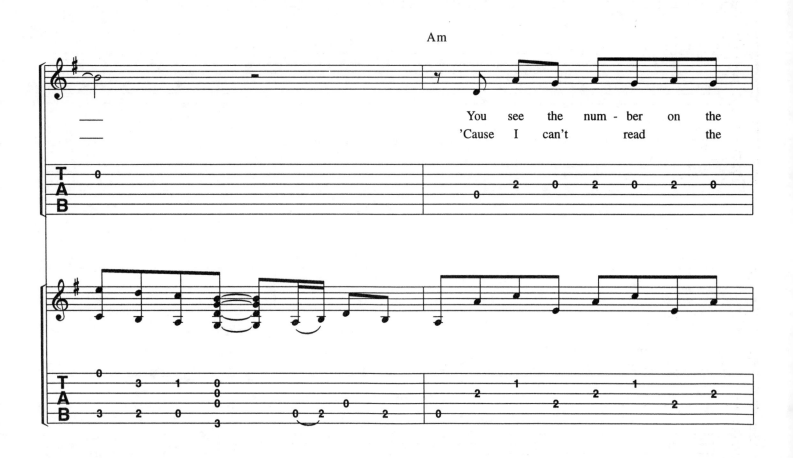

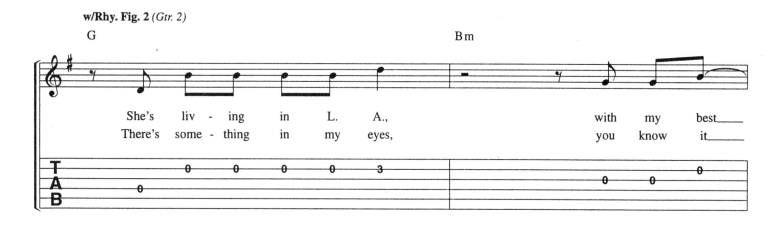

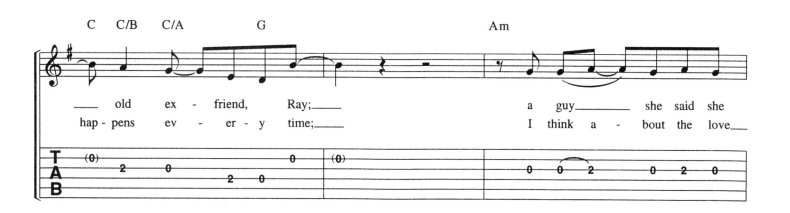

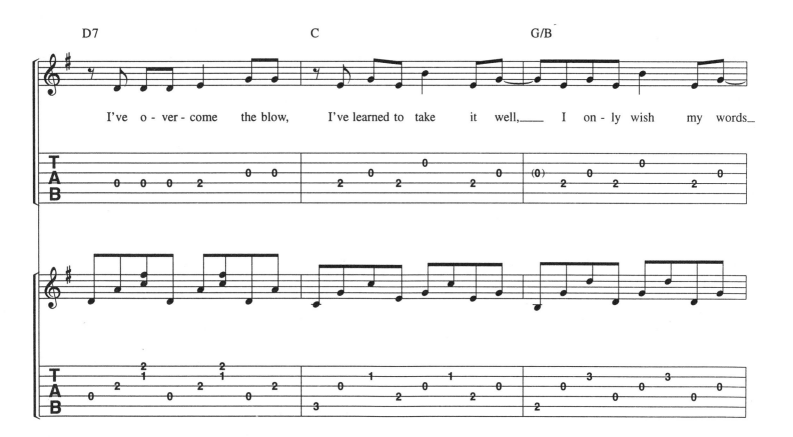

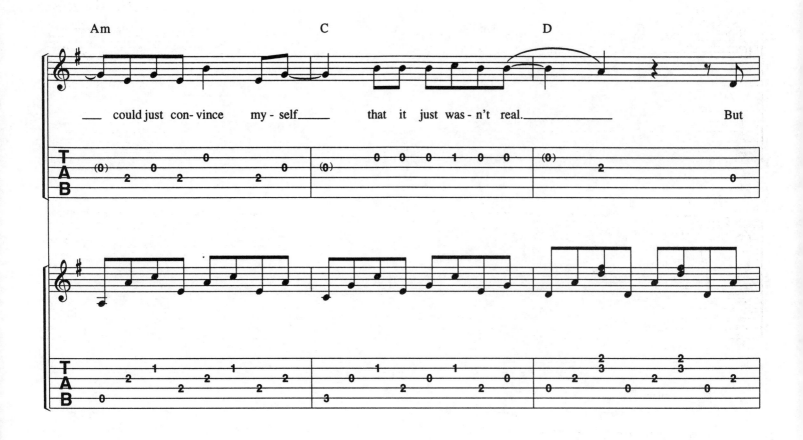

could just con- vince my - self____ that it just was - n't real._____ But

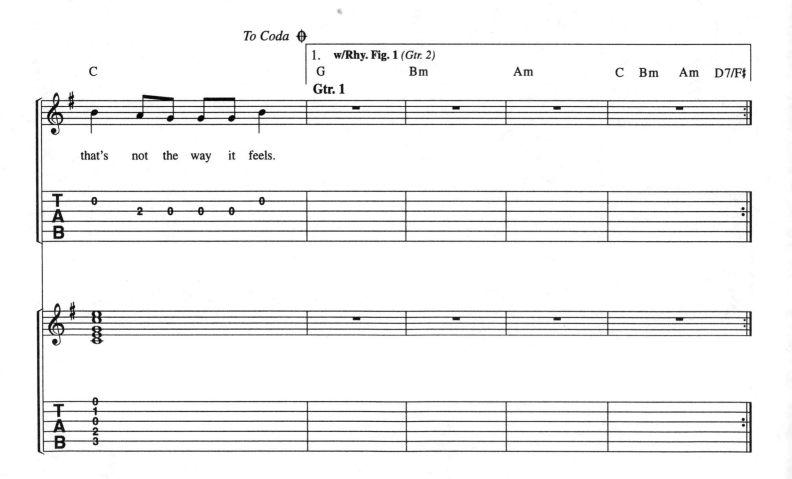

To Coda ⊕

1. **w/Rhy. Fig. 1** *(Gtr. 2)*

that's not the way it feels.

71

Verse 3:
Operator, oh let's forget about this call.
(There's) no one there I really wanted to talk to.
Thank you for your time,
Oh, you've been so much more than kind,
You can keep your dime.
(To Chorus:)

PEOPLE ARE STRANGE

Words and Music by
THE DOORS

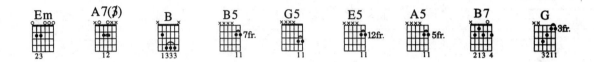

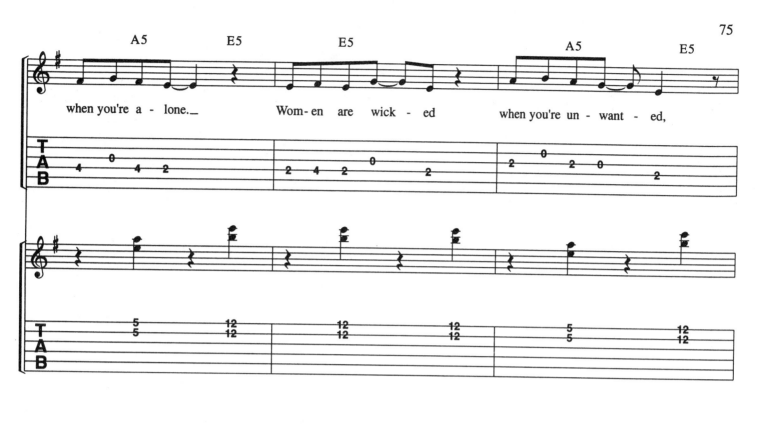

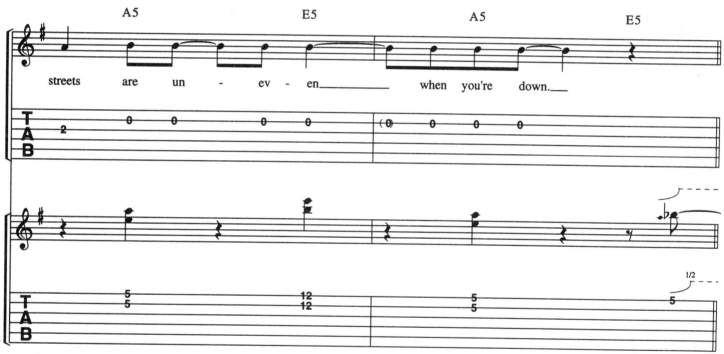

Guitar Solo:

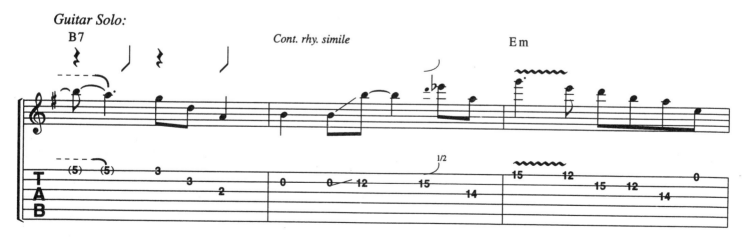

People Are Strange - 6 - 6

*Gradually pull up on bar.

PROUD MARY

by J.C. FOGERTY

C   A   G   F   F6   D   Bm

32 1   213   3211   3241   132   13421

Moderate rock ♩ =126

Intro:

C   A   G   C   A   G   C   A   G   F

F6   F   D   D

Verse:

D *Cont. rhy. simile*

1. Left a good job_____ in the cit _____ y,
2. Cleaned a lot of_____ plates in Mem - phis,
3. If you come down_____ to the riv - er,

work - in' for the man_____ ev - 'ry night and day._____
pumped a lot of pain_____ down in New Or - leans._____
bet you're gon - na find_____ some peo - ple who live._____

And I nev - er lost_____ one min - ute of sleep - in',
But I nev - er saw_____ the good_____ side of the cit - y,
You don't have to wor - ry_____ 'cause_____ you have no mon - ey,

Proud Mary - 4 - 1

Guitar Solo:

SANDMAN

Words and Music by
DEWEY BUNNELL

Moderately slow ♩ = 65

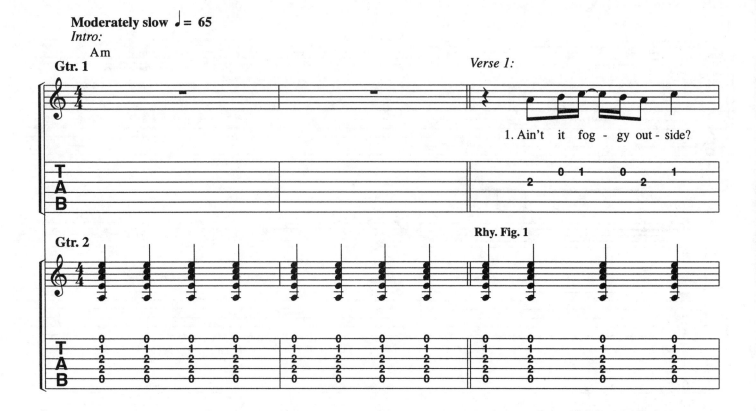

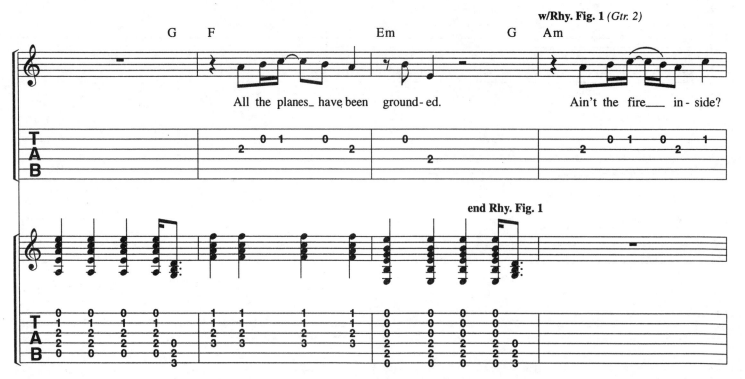

Sandman - 3 - 1

STAIRWAY TO HEAVEN

Words and Music by
JIMMY PAGE and ROBERT PLANT

Slowly ♩ = 72

*Acoustic fingerstyle.

Stairway to Heaven – 11 – 1

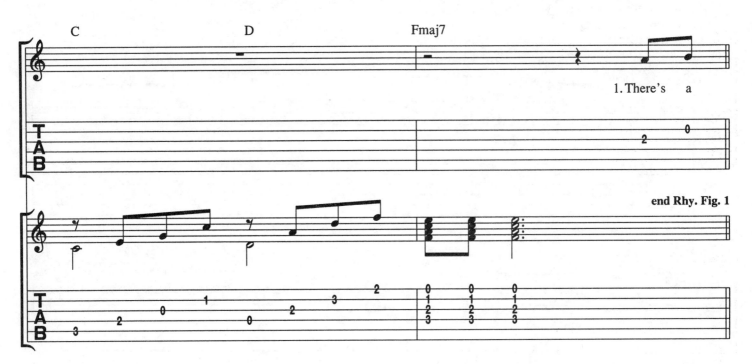

Verse 1:

w/Rhy. Fig. 1 *(Gtr. 1) simile*

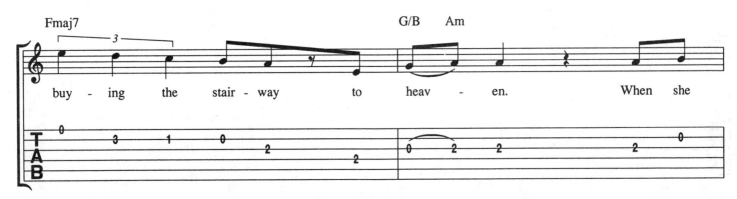

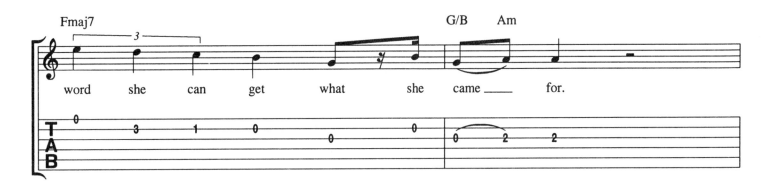

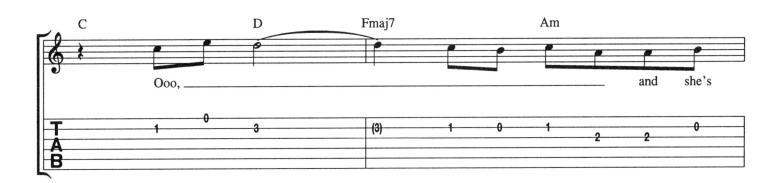

Stairway to Heaven – 11 – 3

Verse 2:

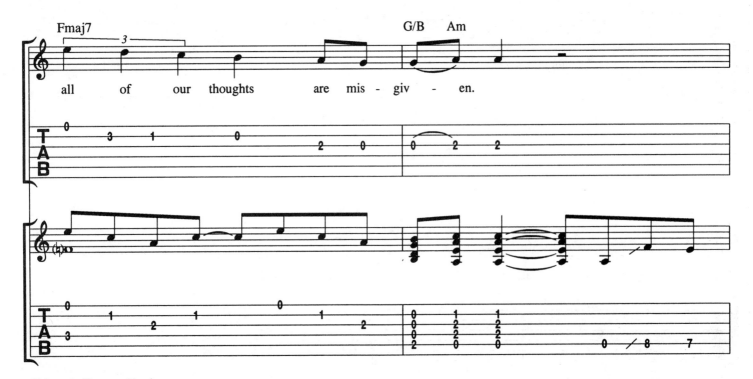

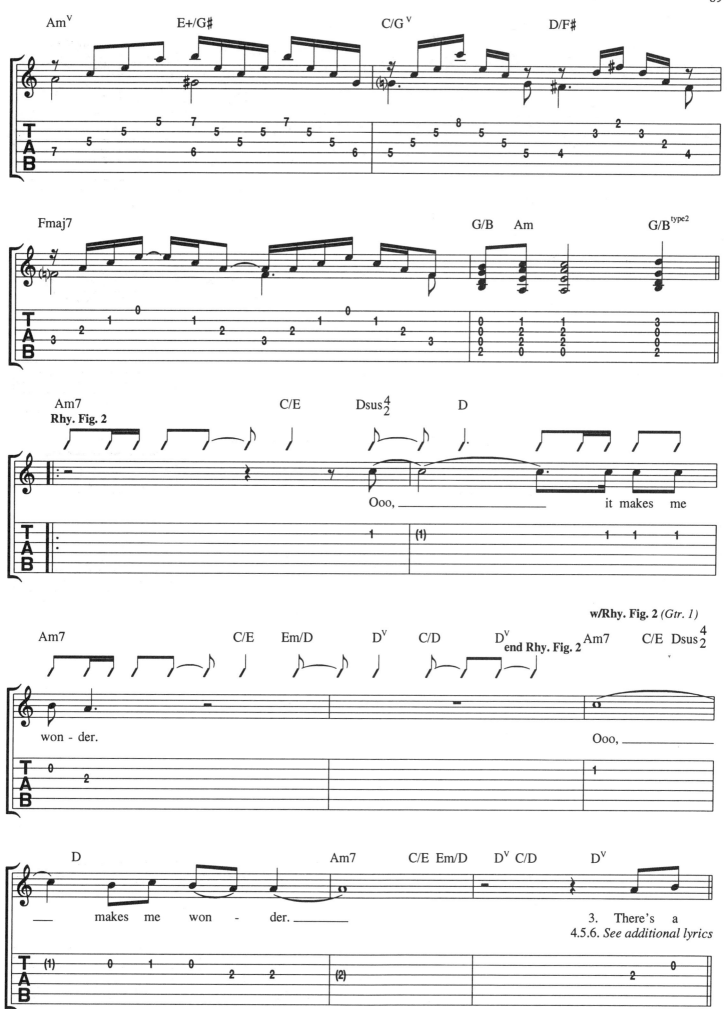

90

Verses 3, 4, 5 & 6:

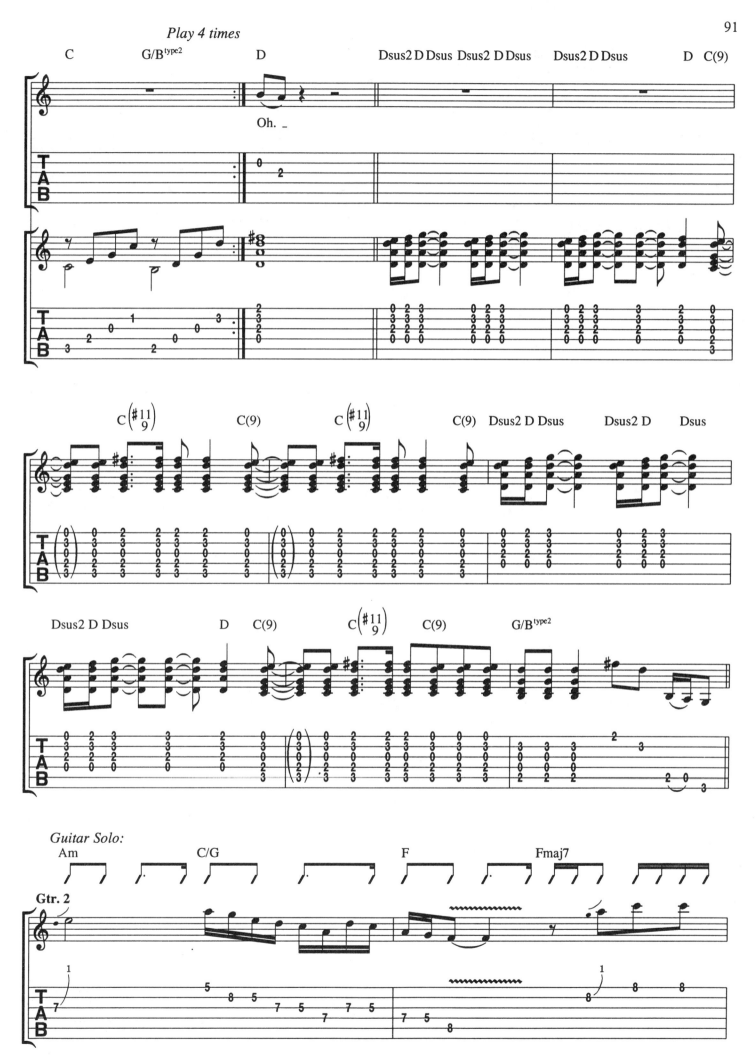

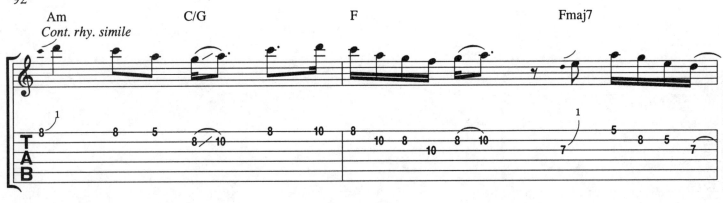

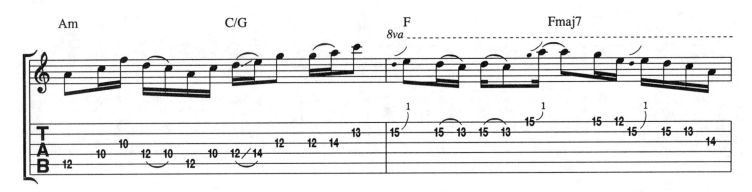

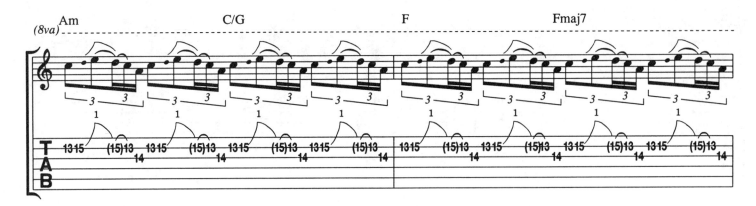

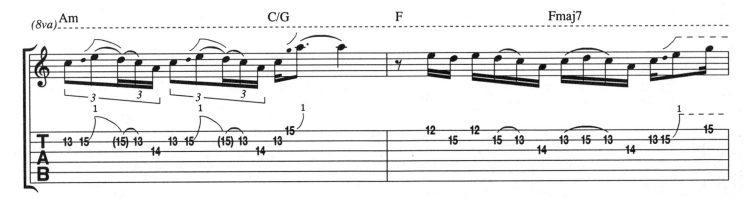

Our shad-ows tall-er than our soul. ___
And if you lis-ten ver-y hard ___

end Rhy. Fig. 3

w/Rhy. Fig. 3 *(Gtr. 2)*

There walks a la-dy we all know, ___
the tune will come ___ to you at last, ___

who shines white light and wants to show. ___
when all are one and one is

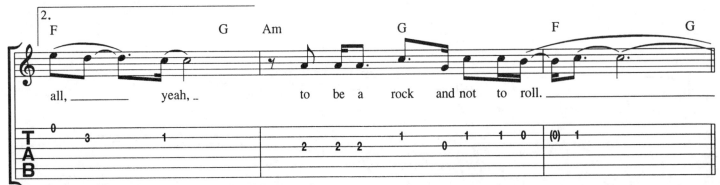

all, ___ yeah, ___ to be a rock and not to roll. ___

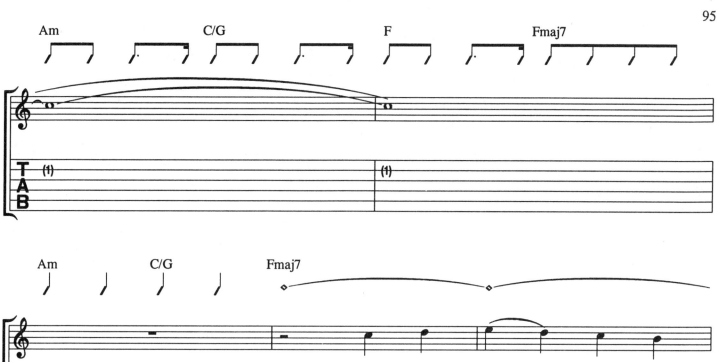

And she's buy - ing a

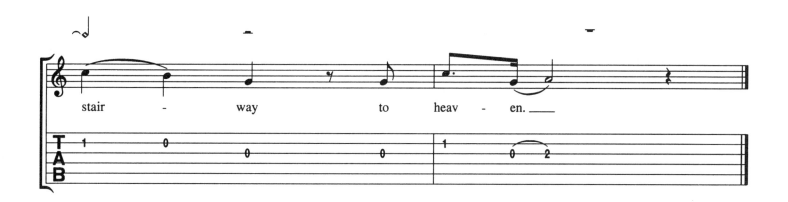

stair - way   to   heav - en. ___

Verse 5:
And it's whispered that soon
If we all call the tune,
Then the piper will lead us to reason.
And a new day will dawn
For those who stand long,
And the forests will echo with laughter.

Verse 6:
If there's a bustle in your hedgerow,
Don't be alarmed now,
It's just a spring clean for the May queen.
Yes, there are two paths you can go by,
But in the long run
There's still time to change the road you're on.

Verse 7:
Your head is humming and it won't go,
In case you don't know
The piper's calling you to join him.
Dear lady, can you hear the wind blow,
And did you know
Your stairway lies on the whispering wind?

TEACH YOUR CHILDREN

Words and Music by
GRAHAM NASH

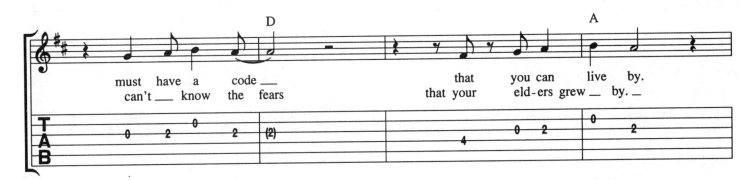

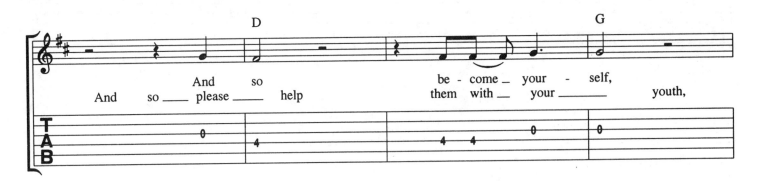

Chorus:

Teach   your chil - dren   well,   their fa - thers'
Teach   your par - ents   well,   the chil - drens'

hell   did slow - ly go ____ by, _____   and
hell   will slow - ly go ____ by, _____

feed   them on ___ your dreams, ___   the one ___ they

picked,   the one ___ you'll know ___ by. _____

Don't you ev - er ask ___ them why,   if they told you, you ___ would

TEQUILA SUNRISE

Words and Music by
DON HENLEY and GLENN FREY

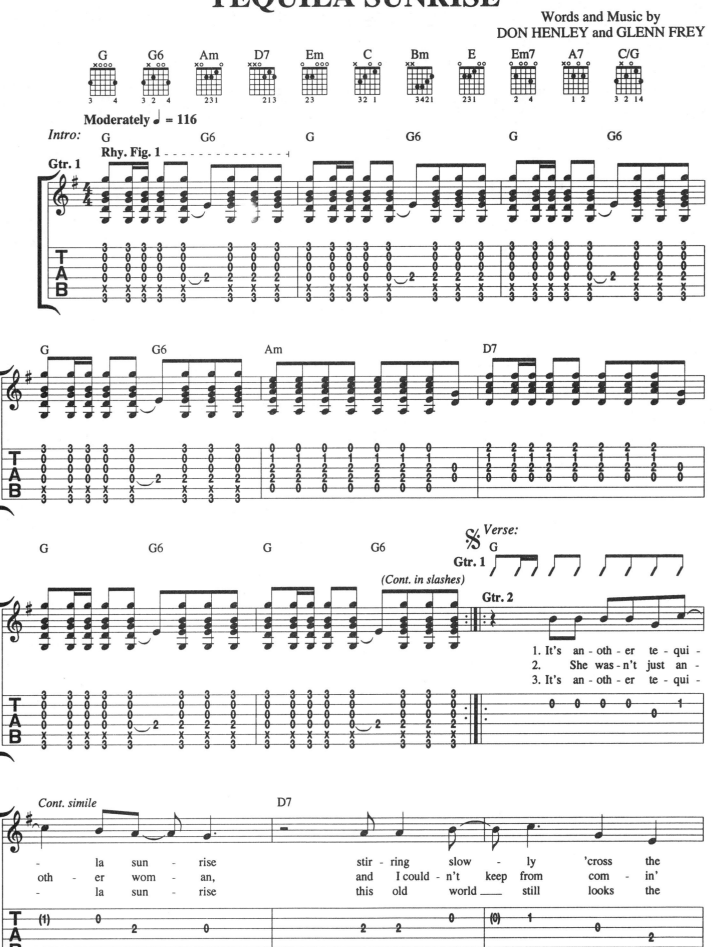

THE NEEDLE AND THE DAMAGE DONE

Words and Music by
NEIL YOUNG

TIME IN A BOTTLE

Words and Music by
JIM CROCE

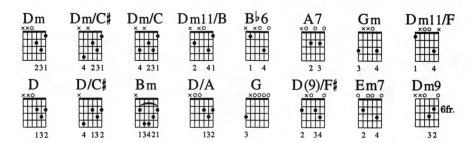

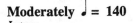

Moderately ♩ = 140
Intro:

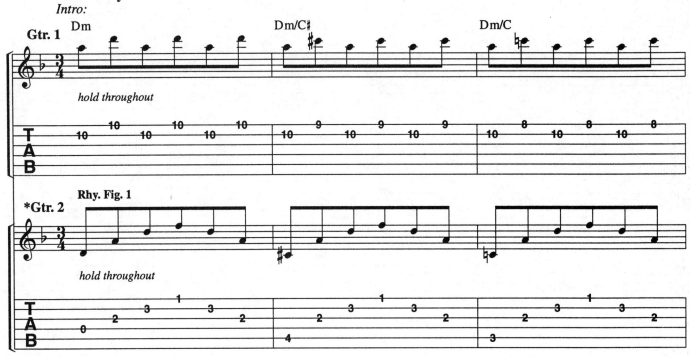

*Gtr. 2 (fingerstyle)

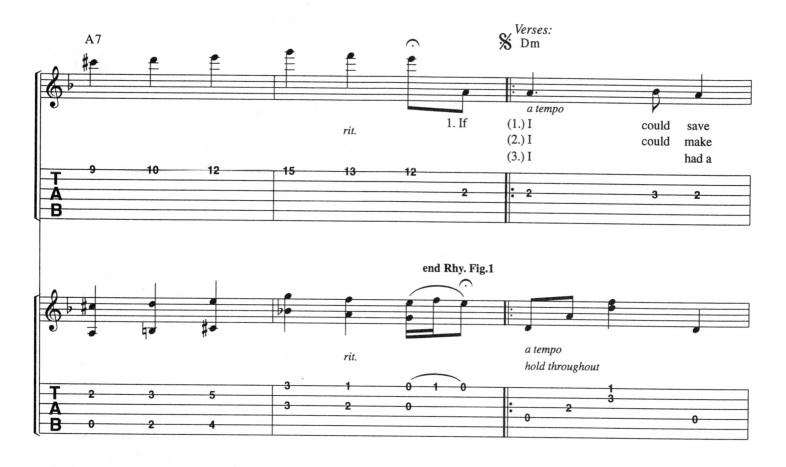

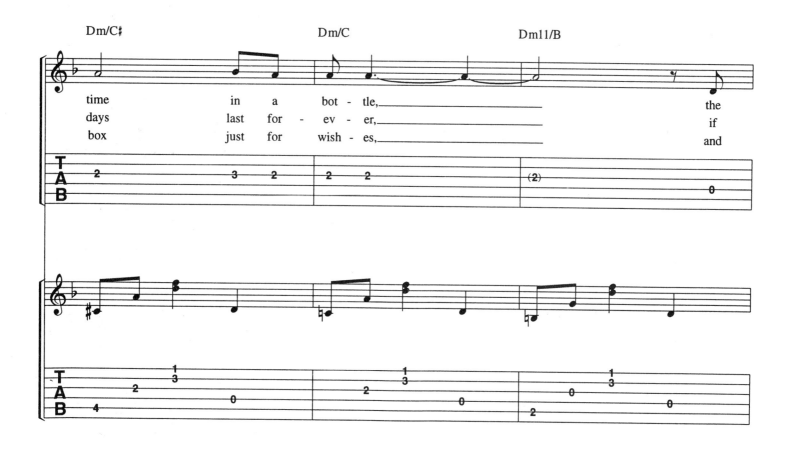

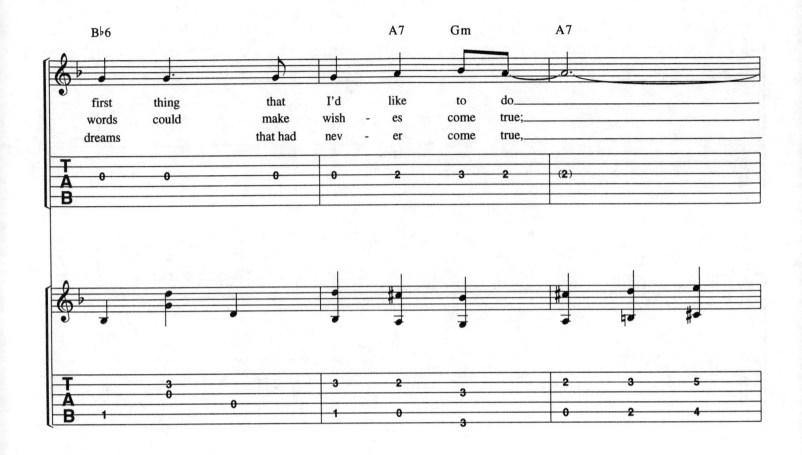

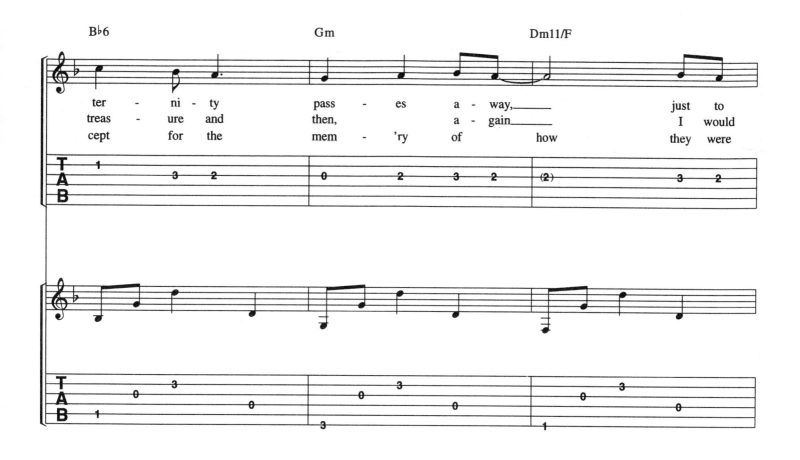

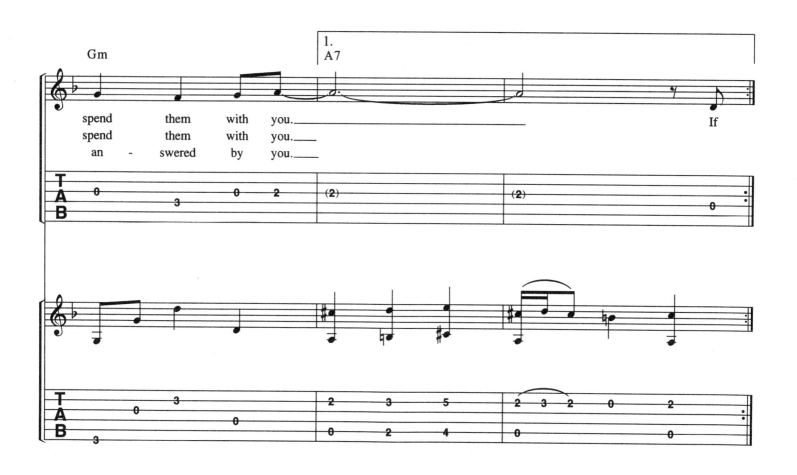

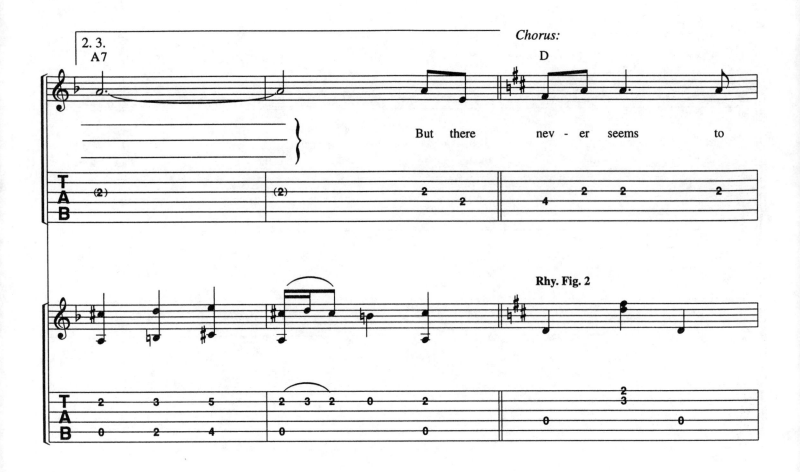

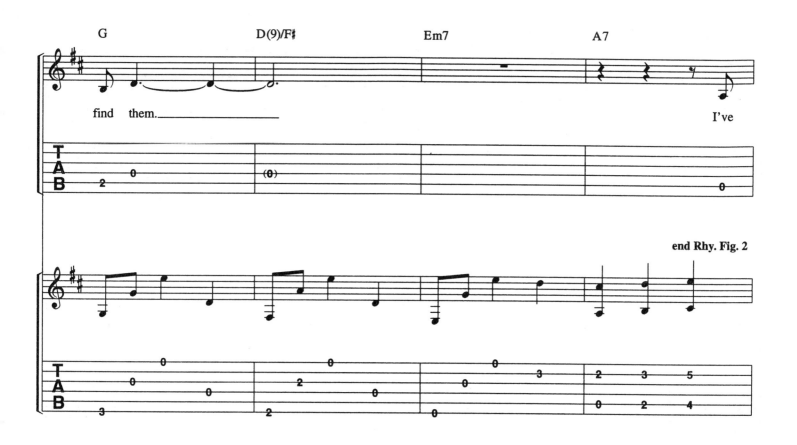

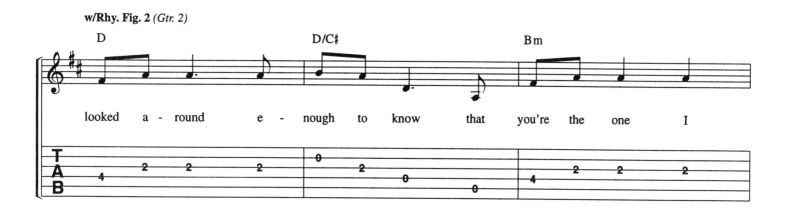

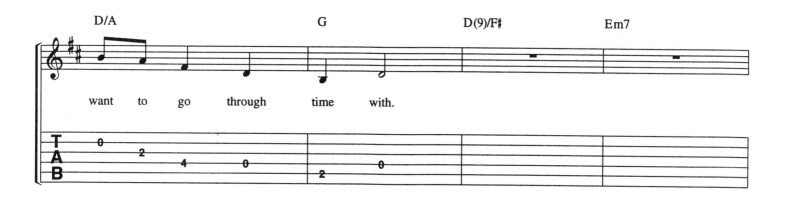

110

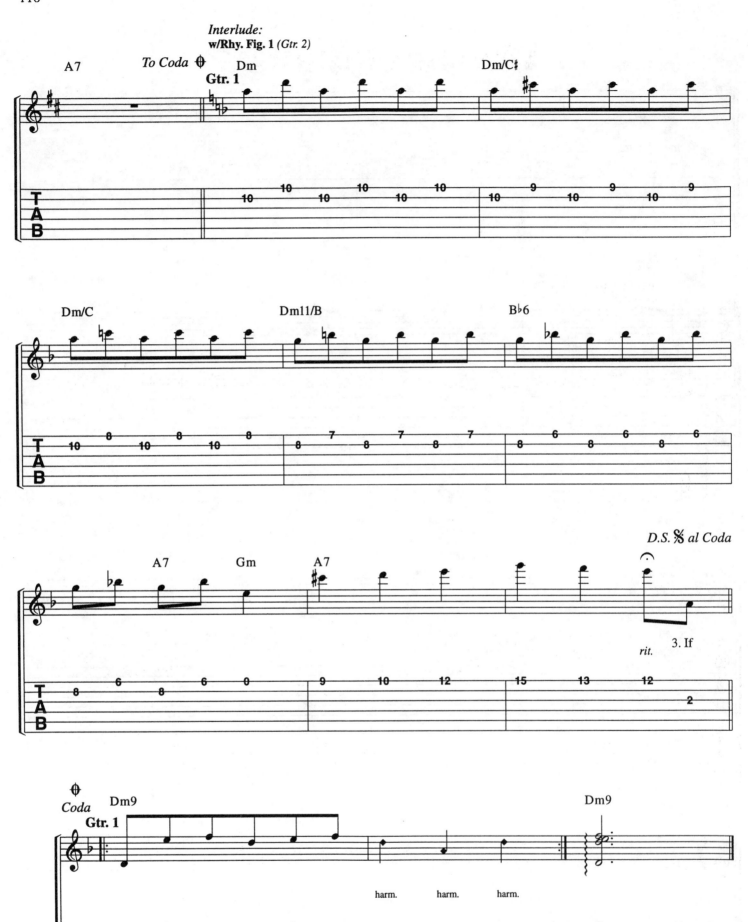

VENTURA HIGHWAY

Words and Music by
DEWEY BUNNELL

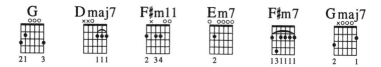

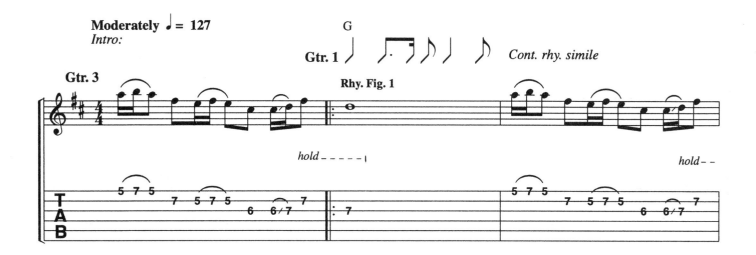

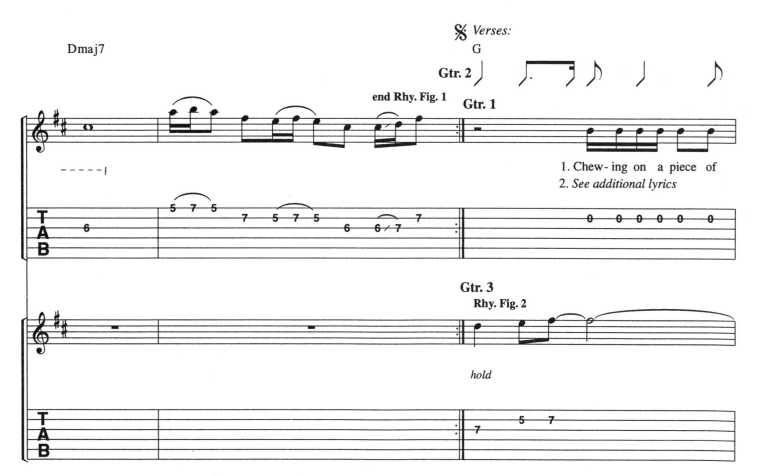

Ventura Highway - 5 - 1

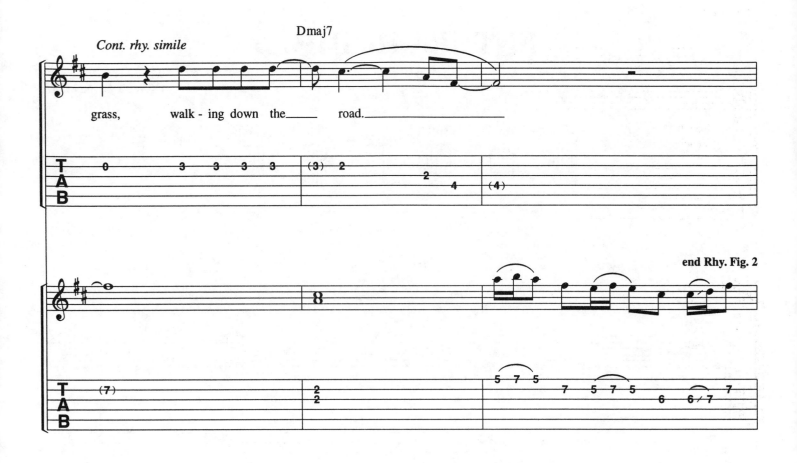

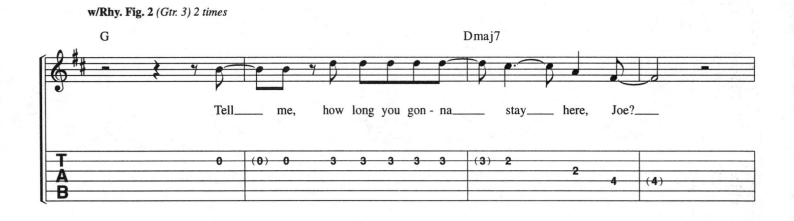

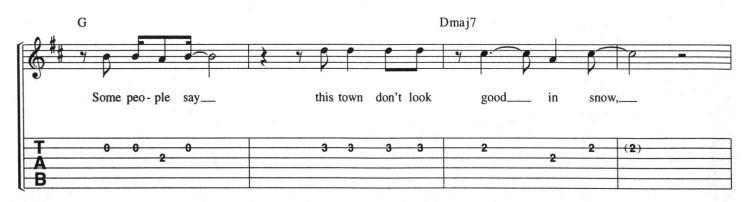

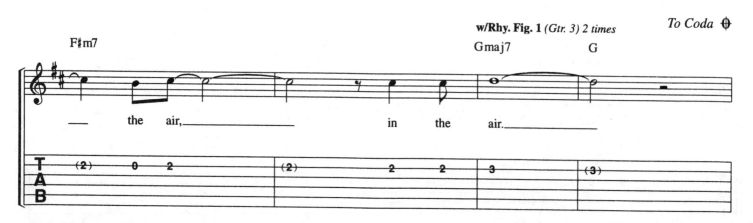

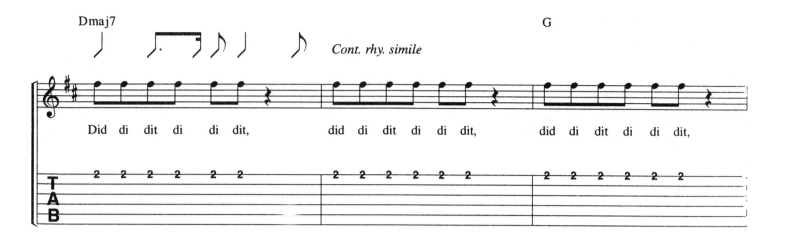

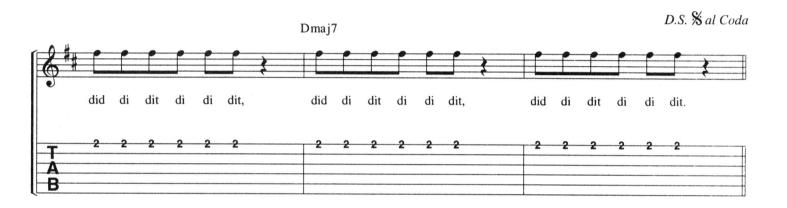

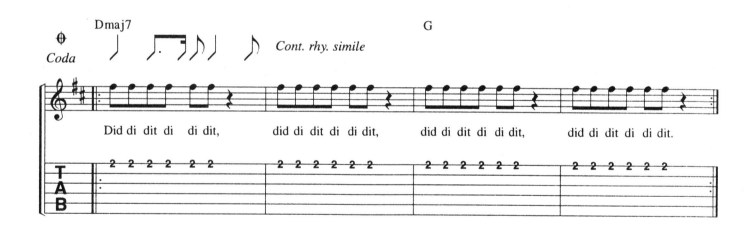

Verse 2:
Wishin' on a falling star,
Waitin' for the early train.
Sorry, boy, but I've been hit by purple rain.
Aw, come on, Joe,
You can always change your name.
Thanks a lot, son, just the same.

TIN MAN

Words and Music by
DEWEY BUNNELL

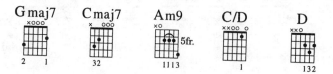

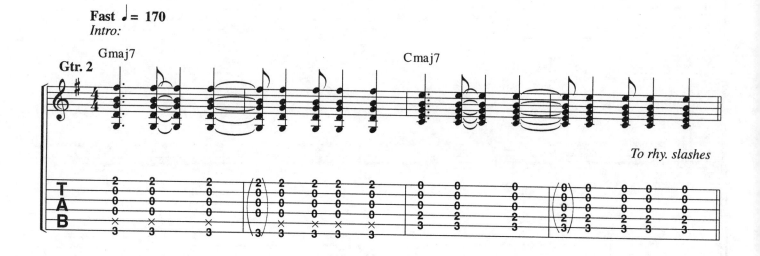

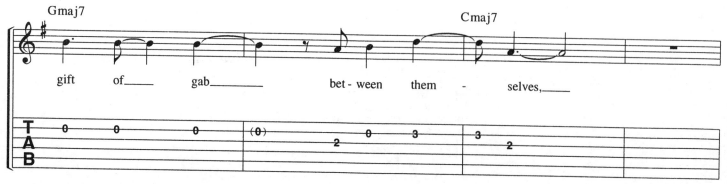

Tin Man - 4 - 1

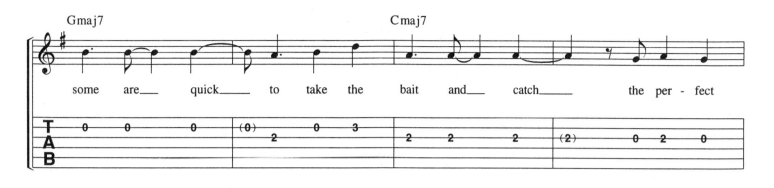

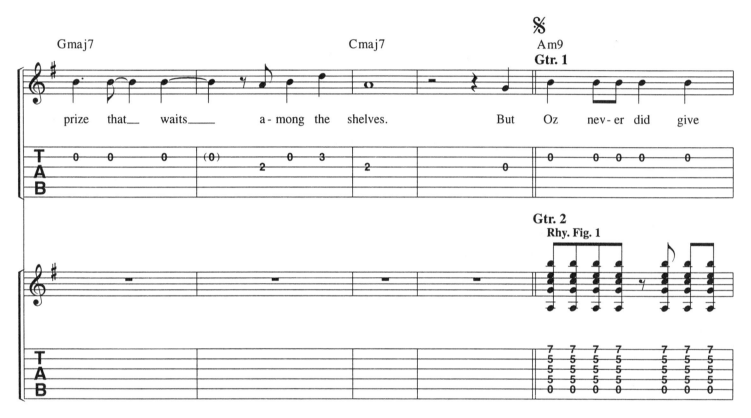

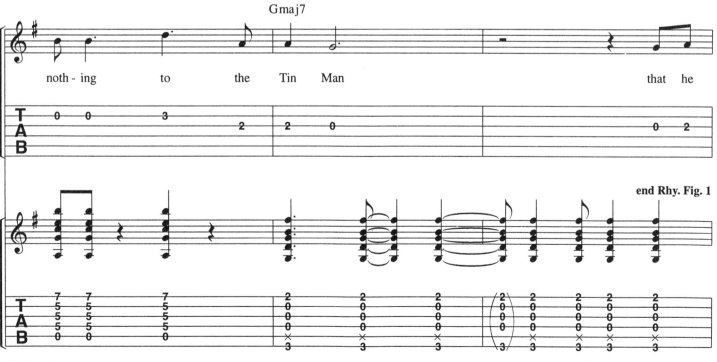

Tin Man - 4 - 2

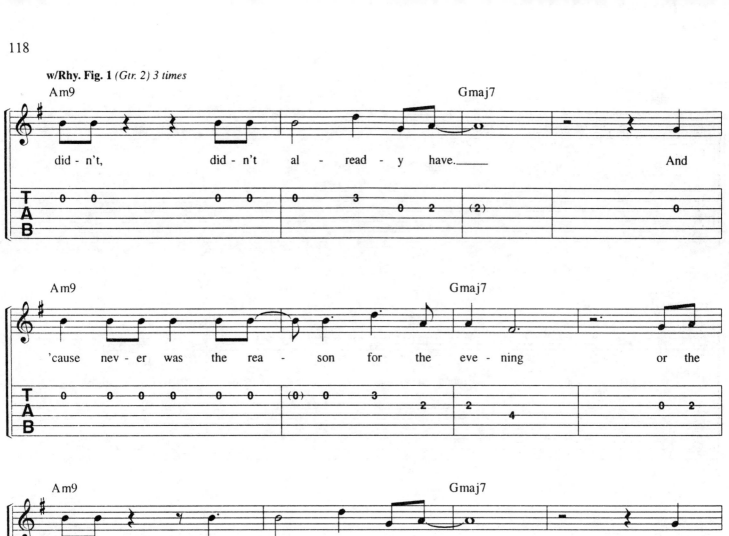

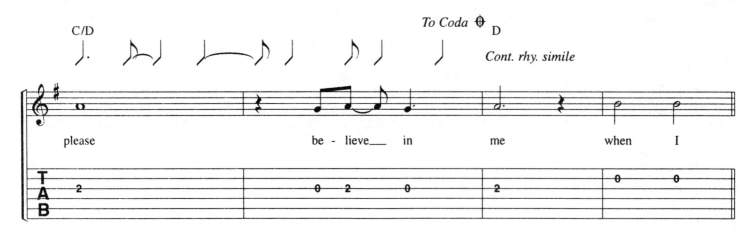

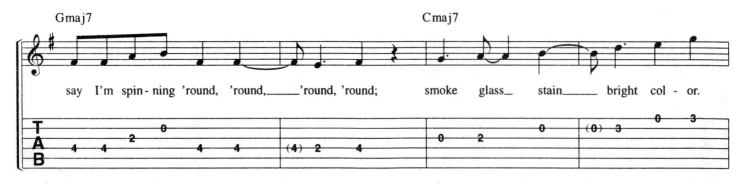

Im - age go - ing down, down,____ down, down; soap - sud____ green____ like bub - bles.

me.

UNCLE JOHN'S BAND

Words by
ROBERT HUNTER
Music by
JERRY GARCIA

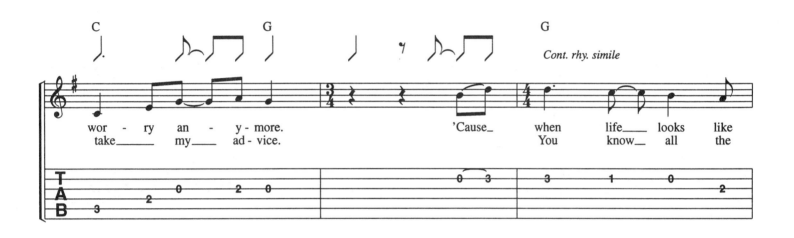

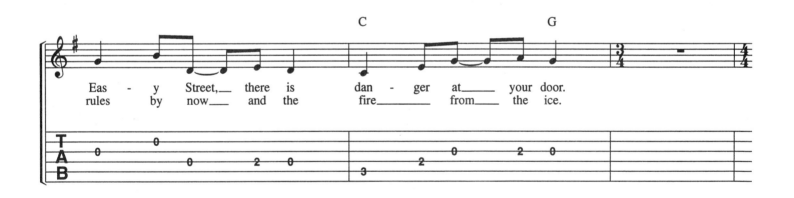

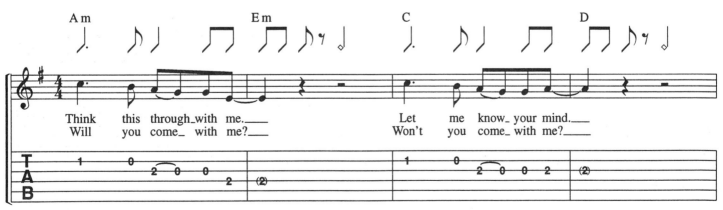

Uncle John's Band - 8 - 2

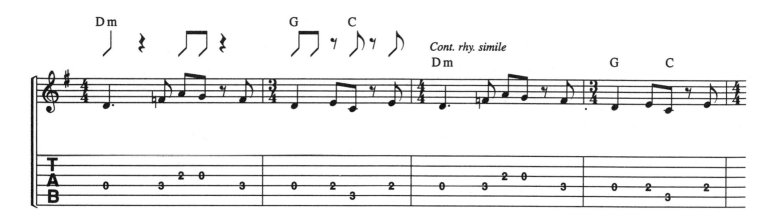

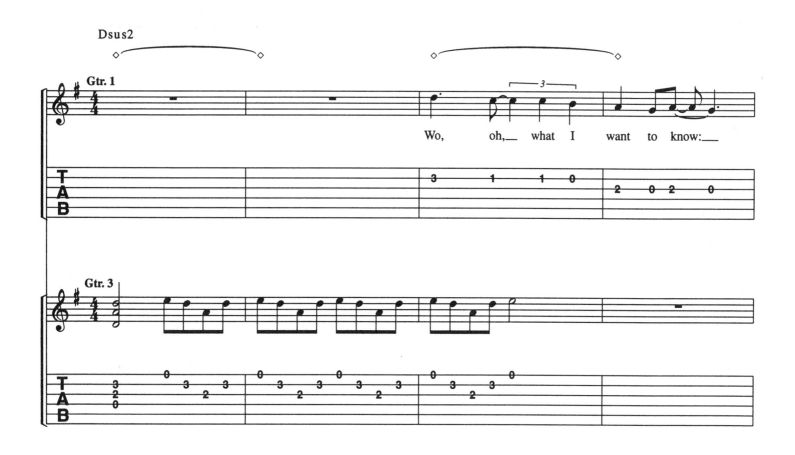

Wo, oh,__ what I want to know:__

How does__ the song go?

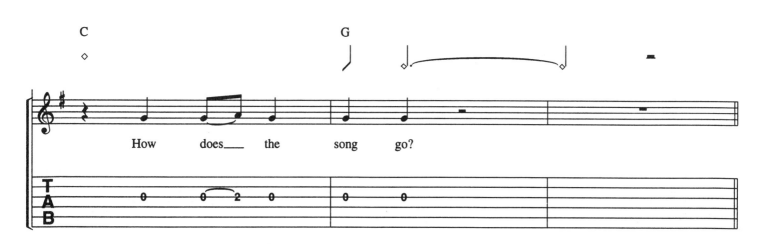

Verse 3:
It's the same story the crow told me,
It's the only one he knows.
Like the morning sun you come
And like the wind you go.
Ain't no time to hate,
Barely time to wait.
Whoa, oh, what I want to know,
Where does the time go?

Verse 4:
I live in a silver mine
And I call it Beggar's tomb.
I got me a violin
And I beg you call the tune.
Anybody's choice,
I can hear you voice.
No, oh, what I want to know,
How does the song go?
(To Chorus:)

GUITAR TAB GLOSSARY **

TABLATURE EXPLANATION

READING TABLATURE: Tablature illustrates the six strings of the guitar. Notes and chords are indicated by the placement of fret numbers on a given string(s).

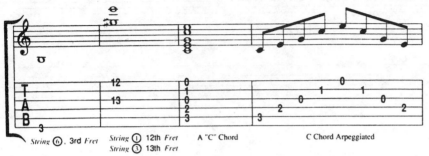

String ⑥, 3rd Fret   String ① 12th Fret   A "C" Chord   C Chord Arpeggiated
String ③ 13th Fret

BENDING NOTES

HALF STEP: Play the note and bend string one half step.*

WHOLE STEP: Play the note and bend string one whole step.

PREBEND AND RELEASE: Bend the string, play it, then release to the original note.

RHYTHM SLASHES

STRUM INDICATIONS: Strum with indicated rhythm. The chord voicings are found on the first page of the transcription underneath the song title.

INDICATING SINGLE NOTES USING RHYTHM SLASHES: Very often single notes are incorporated into a rhythm part. The note name is indicated above the rhythm slash with a fret number and a string indication.

*A half step is the smallest interval in Western music; it is equal to one fret. A whole step equals two frets.

**By Kenn Chipkin and Aaron Stang

ARTICULATIONS

HAMMER ON: Play lower note, then "hammer on" to higher note with another finger. Only the first note is attacked.

PULL OFF: Play higher note, then "pull off" to lower note with another finger. Only the first note is attacked.

LEGATO SLIDE: Play note and slide to the following note. (Only first note is attacked).

PALM MUTE: The note or notes are muted by the palm of the pick hand by lightly touching the string(s) near the bridge.

ACCENT: Notes or chords are to be played with added emphasis.

DOWN STROKES AND UPSTROKES: Notes or chords are to be played with either a downstroke (⊓) or upstroke (∨) of the pick.